Contents

Moving about

People move in many different ways. We wave our arms around. We stand up and use our legs to walk and run. We hop and skip, jump and climb. We swim in water, too.

4

Start Reading
AND LISTENING

How Do We Move?

Sally Morgan

First published in the UK in 2005 by
QED Publishing
A Quarto Group company
226 City Road
London EC1V 2TT
www.qed-publishing.co.uk

A Catalogue record for this book is available from the British Library.

ISBN 1 84538 438 5

Written by Sally Morgan
Designed by Melissa Alaverdy
Editor Hannah Ray
Picture Researcher Nic Dean
Illustrated by Chris Davidson

Series Consultant Anne Faundez
Publisher Steve Evans
Creative Director Louise Morley
Editorial Manager Jean Coppendale

Printed and bound in China

Picture credits

Key: t = top, b = bottom, m = middle, l = left, r = right

Corbis/Larry Williams title page, 17, 21b, /Jim Cummins 5, /Patrik Giardino 9, /Dimitri lundt 11, 20t, /Don Mason 12, /Owen Franken 13, /Michael Wong 14, /Charles Gupton 15, 20b; **Getty Images**/David Madison/Photographer's Choice 4, Nick Clements 6, /Miquel Salmeron/The Image Bank 10.

How many other ways
of moving can you name?

Our skeleton

There are **bones** inside our body. Can you feel the bones in your arms? There are long bones in your arms and legs, and short bones in your hands and feet.

Can you feel the bones in your feet?

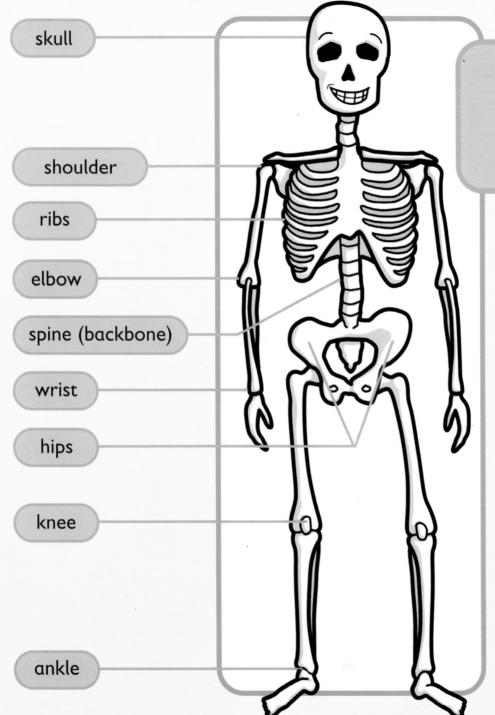

skull

shoulder

ribs

elbow

spine (backbone)

wrist

hips

knee

ankle

Your skeleton is made up of many different bones.

Bones are part of the **skeleton**. Your skeleton **supports** and **protects** your body. Without a skeleton, your body would be like jelly.

7

Muscles

Bones cannot move on their own. They have to be moved by **muscles**. Muscles are attached to bones. When a muscle gets shorter and fatter, it pulls on the bone and makes it move.

biceps

triceps

The bicep muscle makes the arm bend, and the tricep muscle pulls the arm straight.

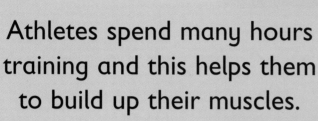
Athletes spend many hours training and this helps them to build up their muscles.

Feel your arm. Now move it around.

Can you feel the muscles moving under your skin?

Walking and running

Babies have to learn how to walk. When we walk, we lift one leg off the ground, move it forwards and put it down. Then we move the other leg in the same way. When we walk, one foot always stays on the ground.

We use powerful muscles in our legs when we run.

When we run, both of our feet may be off the ground at the same time.

11

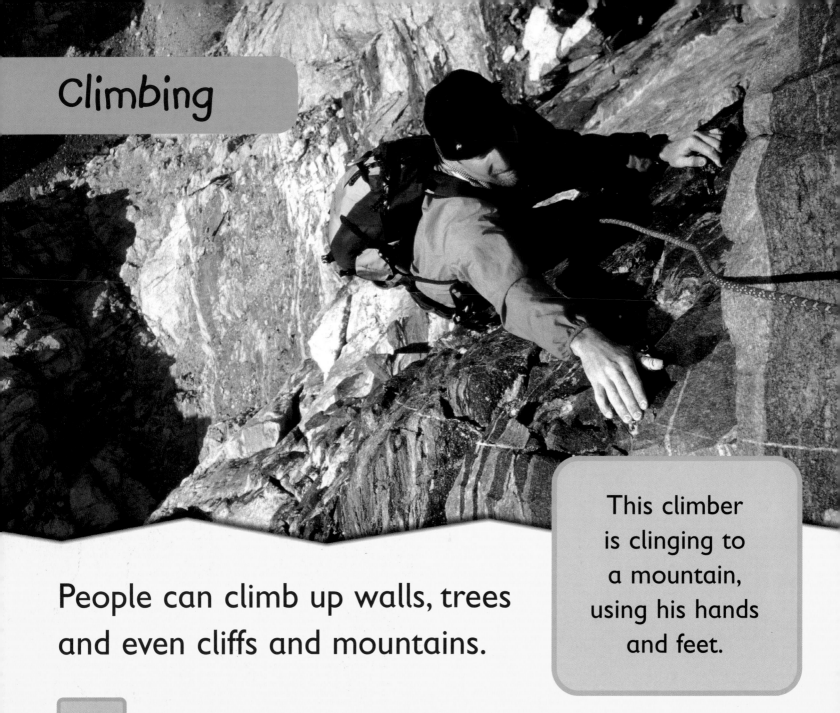

Climbing

People can climb up walls, trees and even cliffs and mountains.

This climber is clinging to a mountain, using his hands and feet.

12

This girl is learning to climb on a specially built wall.

We use our arms and legs to climb. When we start to climb, we stretch out our arms and grip with our hands. We pull our body upwards using our arms. Then we push up with our legs.

13

Jumping and hopping

When we jump, we push our bodies off the ground using our legs. We can jump high in the air or low over the ground. If we run and then jump, we can leap even further.

Hopping is jumping up
and down on one leg.
Can you hop?

Swimming

When we swim, we use our arms and legs to push our bodies through the water.

Can you swim?

We swim by pulling our arms through the water and kicking with our feet.

We can dive and swim underwater, too. When we swim below the surface, we have to hold our breath because we cannot breathe underwater.

What are our skeletons made up of?

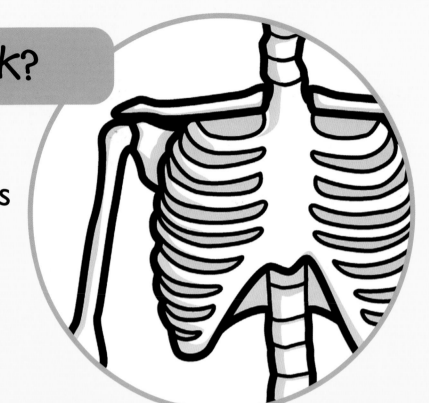

Bones cannot move on their own. What moves your bones?

18

Where in
your body
is your spine?

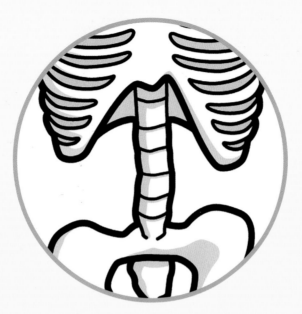

What is the name
of the bone that
surrounds and
protects your brain?

What is the
difference between
walking and running?

How many legs do
we use for hopping?

What do we use our hands for when we are climbing?

Why do we have to hold our breath when we swim underwater?

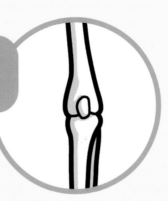

bone – the hard parts of your body that form the skeleton.

muscles – the fleshy parts of your body that move the bones.

protect – to keep something safe.

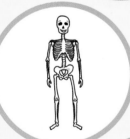

skeleton – the bony framework of a person or animal.

support – to hold something so that it does not fall down.

Index

Parents' and teachers' notes

- Use the glossary and the index to play a simple word game with your child. Ask questions such as 'What does the word bone mean?', 'Which page would you look at to find out about swimming?'

- Read out the text on a type of movement. Ask your child to demonstrate that movement, for example walking or hopping. As your child moves, describe what he/she is doing. Then swap over. Move in a different way (running, jumping, etc.) and encourage your child to describe the way in which you are moving. If your child finds this difficult, ask questions to act as prompts, e.g. 'What are my feet doing?', 'Am I moving my arms or hands?'

- Ask your child to see how far he/she can jump. Mark a point on the ground and ask your child to jump from standing still. Measure the distance he/she jumped. Then, ask your child to take another jump, this time with a run up. Measure this distance. What is the difference in measurement? Look up the world record long jump distance and compare the distance with that jumped by your child.

- Watch a sports programme on the television and ask your child to identify different types of movement such as walking, running and jumping. Watch athletics events such as pole-vaulting and ask your child how the athletes manage to jump so high.

- Ask your child to describe how he/she would climb a tree and the parts of the body he/she would use.

- If your child can swim, ask him/her about the different types of strokes. How do we move our bodies differently when doing different strokes?

- Can your child skip? Go outside and skip with a skipping rope. How do we skip? Watch each other skip and see which bits of our bodies we use. Then, together, write a page about skipping that could be included in another book about movement.

- The text in this book does not cover the issue of disability. When talking to your child about moving, bring up the subject of disability and how a disabled person may be able to move about. Talk about the Paralympics and the fact that disabled people can become top athletes.

24